Caterpillars

Caterpillars

Patrick Merrick

THE CHILD'S WORLD®, INC.

Library of Congress Cataloging-in-Publication Data
Merrick, Patrick.
Caterpillars/Patrick Merrick.
p.   cm.
Includes index.
Summary: Describes the physical characteristics, habitat, behavior, and life cycle of caterpillars.
ISBN 1-56766-380-X (lib. bdg.)
1. Caterpillars—Juvenile literature. [1. Caterpillars.
2. Butterflies—Metamorphosis. 3. Metamorphosis.] I. Title
QL544.2.M47   1997
595.78'139—dc21   96-46956
                                CIP
                                AC

Photo Credits

DPA/DEMBINSKY PHOTO ASSOC: 23
Gijsbert van Frankenhuyzen/DEMBINSKY PHOTO ASSOC: 29
Gary Meszaros/DEMBINSKY PHOTO ASSOC: 20
Joe McDonald: 16
Robert and Linda Mitchell: 15
Rod Planck/DEMBINSKY PHOTO ASSOC: 2, 10
Sharon Cummings/DEMBINSKY PHOTO ASSOC: 19, 30
Skip Moody/DEMBINSKY PHOTO ASSOC: 9, 13, 24, 26
Stan Osolinski/DEMBINSKY PHOTO ASSOC: 6
Bill Ivy/Tony Stone Images: cover

On the cover...

Front cover: A *luna caterpillar* climbs on a twig.
Page 2: A *cecropia caterpillar* has a brightly colored head.

Table of Contents

Is your backyard full of wild and strange animals? At first glance, you might not think so. But if you look closer, you'll see lots of animal life! Beautiful birds fly overhead. Squirrels race up the trees. Rabbits hop across the lawn. But some of the most exciting animals are the ones you have to search for—like grasshoppers, dragonflies, moths, ladybugs, and other creepy, crawly creatures. And one of the most interesting is the caterpillar.

A *cecropia moth caterpillar* climbs up a branch.

What Do Caterpillars Look Like?

A caterpillar is a kind of baby **insect**. An insect is an animal with six legs. It also has three separate parts to its body—head, **thorax** and **abdomen**. The thorax is the chest of an insect and the abdomen is the stomach. Most baby insects look like little worms. They are called **larva**. A caterpillar is a larval butterfly or moth.

There are many different kinds of butterflies and moths in the world. In fact, there are over 112,000 different kinds! These different kinds are called **species**. Each species has its own kind of caterpillar.

A *pandora sphinx caterpillar* climbs on a twig.

A caterpillar has a mouth that is perfect for chewing leaves. Its jaws move like pliers to rip the leaf apart. It also has many tiny eyes. Caterpillars can't see very well, but they can tell the difference between light and dark.

Caterpillars are soft and round. They can be as big as seven inches long or as small as one-tenth of an inch. They can be any color of the rainbow. Many of them are smooth, but some of them are hairy. In fact, the word caterpillar means "hairy cat"!

These *monarch butterfly caterpillars* are eating milkweed leaves.

What Are Caterpillars' Legs Like?

Caterpillars have short, fat legs. These legs are strong enough to hold up a long, heavy abdomen. Each leg ends in a hook. The hooks help the caterpillar hold onto plants. To move their long bodies and all those legs, caterpillars have lots of different muscles—over 2,000 of them! That's four times as many muscles as you have.

This cecropia caterpillar uses its feet to hold on to a branch.

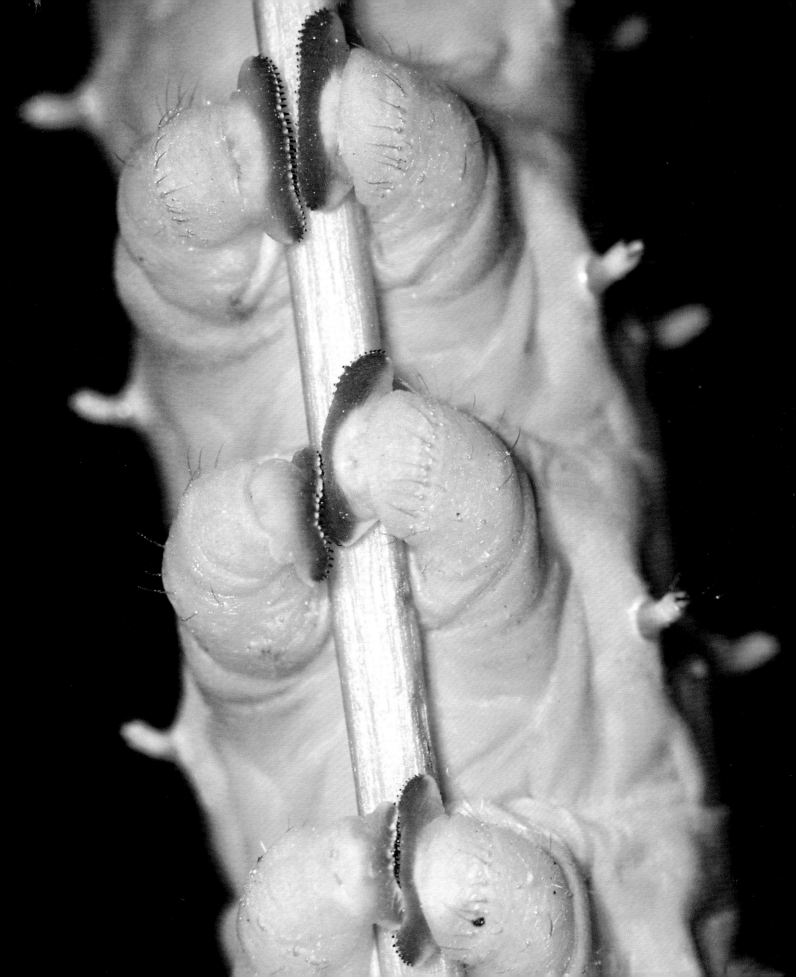

What Do Caterpillars Eat?

All caterpillars eat leaves, but many are fussy eaters. Some eat the leaves of only one type of plant. The monarch butterfly caterpillar eats only milkweed plants. Other caterpillars eat only the leaves from a certain family of plants. The *cabbage moth caterpillar* eats only plants in the cabbage family. The cabbage family includes cabbage, cauliflower, and broccoli.

This *Eastern black swallowtail caterpillar* is eating the leaves off a branch.

Do Caterpillars Have Enemies?

The slow-moving caterpillar has many enemies. Birds, lizards, rodents, and even other insects like to eat caterpillars. These hunting animals are called **predators**.

Caterpillars have found ways to protect themselves from predators. Some caterpillars protect themselves by looking like something else. This ability is called **camouflage**. Some caterpillars use camouflage to hide against their surroundings. The *orange-dog swallowtail caterpillar* looks like bird droppings on a leaf. Others use camouflage to make themselves look scarier. The *tiger swallowtail caterpillar* has fake eye spots on its back. This caterpillar's enemies don't know if it is coming or going!

The large spots on this swallowtail caterpillar look like eyes.

Some caterpillars even sounds to frighten away predators. The *sphinx moth caterpillar* squeaks loudly if it is attacked. Some caterpillars even scare their enemies with nasty odors! The *black swallowtail caterpillar* smells like a dead animal.

This black swallowtail caterpillar is hanging from a branch.

Are Caterpillars Poisonous?

Almost all caterpillars are harmless. But about 50 types of caterpillars protect themselves by using poison! Two common poisonous caterpillars live in the United States. They are the *Io moth caterpillar* and the *saddle-back caterpillar*. Both of these caterpillars have poisonous **venom** in their sharp spikes. The venom causes stinging and swelling.

The sharp spikes on this saddle-back caterpillar are full of venom.

Where Do Caterpillars Lay Eggs?

When a female butterfly or moth is ready to lay her eggs, she flies among the trees and bushes to find the right place. She must lay her eggs on the right kind of plant so her babies will have food. When she finds the right plant, she lays the eggs.

Butterflies usually lay one or two eggs on each leaf. Then they fly off and leave them. Moths usually lay a large number of eggs in one spot. Then the moths try to hide the eggs with hair or scales. Some eggs hatch quickly, but others take longer. The eggs of monarch butterflies hatch in only three days. The eggs of *gypsy moths* take three months to hatch.

Cecropia caterpillar eggs lay in a row.

When a caterpillar hatches, the only thing it wants to do is eat. As it eats, it gets bigger. The caterpillar has a hard, shell-like skin. When it gets too big for its skin, it gets rid of it! This is called **molting**. Underneath the old skin there is a new, bigger skin. The caterpillar molts up to six times before it becomes an adult.

When the caterpillar has grown as big as it can, it stops eating. Then it searches for a safe place where it can turn into a moth or butterfly. When it finds the right place, it starts forming a case, or **cocoon**, around itself. The cocoon is made of silk that the caterpillar makes inside its body.

This monarch butterfly caterpillar has just finished molting.

While it is in its cocoon, the caterpillar is called a **pupa**. The pupa's tiny body parts break down and rebuild themselves into butterfly parts. This would be like taking a bicycle apart and using the parts to make a hang glider! The pupa usually stays in its cocoon for the entire winter.

This monarch butterfly is ready to come out of its cocoon.

How Do Caterpillars Use Silk?

All caterpillars form their cocoons by spinning silk. The silk is made by special body parts that are shaped like springs. These curly body parts are very large. If they were stretched out, they would be up to five times as long as the whole caterpillar!

Some caterpillars use silk for more than just making cocoons. They also use it to escape from predators! *Tent caterpillars* build huge silk nests and hide in them during the day. *Leaf-roller caterpillars* tie silk around leaves to protect themselves. *Inchworm caterpillars* connect their silk to a tree branch. When a predator comes by, they just fall off the branch and swing away!

Silk nests made by tent caterpillars cover some trees.

Caterpillars are strange and wonderful creatures. Since they live all over the world, they are easy to find. They can make fun pets—just be careful not to touch fuzzy caterpillars! If you want to keep a caterpillar, remember exactly where you found it. Then you can feed it fresh leaves from the same plant. Soon, you might end up with a beautiful moth or butterfly to set free!

Tussock caterpillars like this one have many bright colors.

Glossary

abdomen (AB-duh-men)
The stomach area of an insect is called an abdomen.

camouflage (KAM-uh-flazh)
When an animal uses camouflage, it hides from enemies by looking like something else. Some caterpillars use camouflage to protect themselves.

cocoon (kuh-KOON)
A cocoon is a case made of silk that a caterpillar forms around itself. Inside the cocoon, the caterpillar turns into a moth or butterfly.

insect (IN-sekt)
An insect is an animal with six legs and a body with three parts.

larva (LAR-vah)
Larvae are baby insects. Caterpillars are larvae.

molting (MOLT-ing)
Getting rid of an old layer of skin is called molting.

predator (PRED-uh-ter)
A predator is an animal that eats other animals. Birds, lizards, and rodents are predators that eat caterpillars.

pupa (PEW-puh)
A caterpillar inside its cocoon is called a pupa.

species (SPEE-sheez)
A species is a separate kind of an animal. There are over 100,000 different species of caterpillars.

thorax (THOR-ax)
The chest area of an adult insect is called a thorax.

venom (VEN-um)
Venom is a poison made by some animals. A few kinds of caterpillars use venom to protect themselves.

Index